ONE HOUSE DOWN

When it comes to one's place of origin, the tides are strong—the pull to hold on, and the push to let go. In this luminous, thoughtful collection, Gianna Russo explores the bittersweet legacies of old Florida. One House Down is rooted rooted deeply in place, whether Nebraska Avenue and Central Avenue, cultural seats such as the Fun-Lan Drive-In and the Sanwa market, or the ripe specificity of "Faedo's Bakery [as] men roll loaves / of Cuban bread, turnovers of guava paste." I appreciate Russo's musicality and her formal agility, as she experiments with ekphrasis, ghazal, pantoum, and pecha kucha. Whether the stubborn advice of the Methodist Women's Society Cookbook, or the dark chuckle of a plaster cat on a funeral home's roof, these are poems we need.

—Sandra Beasley, author of *Count the Waves*

Gianna Russo's poetry captures life in her Tampa neighborhood, and perhaps neighborhoods everywhere, in all its glory and horror – it's where good people and bad people love and hate, eat bacon and eggs, die by gunshot, listen to the rattle of swaying palms and the cries of night birds. Folks sweat and bleed, cry and laugh. I don't think a story of a neighborhood has ever been told so well. I am grateful for this wonderful work.

—Jeff Klinkenberg, author of *Son of Real Florida: Stories from my Life* and recipient of the Florida Humanities Council Lifetime Achievement Award for Writing

Gianna Russo's *One House Down* shows a poet of true lyricism and storytelling gifts and remarkable range. A Tampa, Florida native, Russo explores being Southern and Italian. She digs out the "other" side of Tampa, the part once chic and that then took a fall to the tawdry. She combines a pastoral "[lying]down into daisy light" with the urban realism of "Pay-Day loans and pawnshops." With elegance, Russo smashes up days past when "Tampa was a 45 record" against "the new interstate" which carved up the old neighborhoods. She reminisces about streets where on one end was "white trash" and on the other end Italians. A childhood presses up against sexuality, racism, hurricanes, and the sumptuous imagery of an almost lost Florida west coast. She embraces all of it with grief, grit, guile and tenderness.

—Mary Jane Ryals, Poet Laureate of the Big Bend of Florida and author of *Cookie and Me*

continued on page 87 . . .

ONE HOUSE DOWN

Poems

GIANNA RUSSO

Lake Dallas, Texas

FIRST EDITION

Requests for permission to reprint or reuse material from this work should be sent to:

Permissions
Madville Publishing
PO Box 358
Lake Dallas, TX 75065

Acknowledgements:

Apalachee Review: "Memory in Green," "Two Houses Down, Middle of the Night" (appeared as "Two Houses Down"), "Methodist Women's Society Cookbook" and "Danny Jackson Must Not Die."
Florida English: "Examining the Cannon."
Florida Review: "So Many Hitchhikers on this Street."
Florida Review, Aquifer: "After the Poetry Reading, a Condom."
Green Mountains Review: "Boutonniere."
Gulf Coast: "Old Orange Avenue" appeared in a slightly different version.
Italian Americana: "Balancing, Truing and Personal Service."
Kestrel: "United Daughters of the Confederacy Float" appeared in a slightly different version.
Negative Capability: "Laundry."
Panoplyzine: "Old South Carriage Tours."
Rebus: "In Sumptious Ticking."
saw palm: "Flood Subject."
Sweet: A Literary Confection: "Somewhere Jazz."
Valparaiso Poetry Review: "Winter Solstice, Paris Street."
Water Stone: "From Sea to Shining."
Zingara: "Reverend Billy's Boogie Woogie and Mom's Gulbransen" and "Please Help This Vet."

"Did You Find Everything You Need?" "Sanwa International Grocery," and "United Daughters of the Confederacy Float" were exhibited as part of the Hambidge Center Sign of the Times exhibit, March-June 2018.

Cover design: Jeff Karon and Kimberly Davis
Cover photo: Gianna Russo
Author photo: Lou Russo.

ISBN: 978-1-948692-20-5 Paper, 978-1-948692-21-2 ebook
Library of Congress Control Number: 2019937658

for Jeff

TABLE OF CONTENTS

Two Houses Down, Middle of the Night   1

*

After the Poetry Reading, a Condom   4
The House Called Shadow Garden   5
Neighborhood Watch   6
At the Royal Palm Motel   7
"Please Help This Vet"   8
Old Orange Avenue   9
Old South Carriage Tours   10
Where Letha Lived   12
I Have Monkeys   15
Men on Bikes: A Standardized Test for
    White Women Alone on the Street   16
Laundry   18
You Didn't Hear It from Me   19
Memory in Green   21
Flood Subject   22
Danny Jackson Must Not Die   23
Night Train and Little Owl   25
Where Shopping is a Pleasure   26
Professional Development: Active Shooter   28
HEADLINE: Student had Gun, Cops Say   29
Politics   30
Balancing, Truing, and Personal Service   31

The Ember of the Nursing Home 32

Nebraska Avenue Torch Song 33

Winter Solstice, Paris Street 34

*

Examining the Cannon 36

Pecha Kucha for Big Guava 37

*

New Year's Eve, Paris Street 48

The Good Samaritan of Florida Avenue 49

In Sumptuous Ticking 51

Still Life 53

In the Midst of Magnolia 54

Sorry About that Thing I Heard 55

American Pantoum 57

Did You Find Everything You Need? 59

Thanksgiving Eve at Family Dollar 60

From Sea to Shining 61

Fairyland 62

Boutonniere 63

Reverend Billy's Boogie Woogie
  and Mom's Gulbransen 64

The Methodist Women's Society Cookbook 65

Best Supporting Role 67

Between Mickey Mouse
  and I Don't Give a Damn 68

Corner of Blanco and South Streets 69

The United Daughters of the Confederacy Float 70

So Many Hitchhikers on this Street 71

Nice 'N' Easy 72

"Anything Helps, God Bless"   73

Walking Home on Hanna Avenue, July 4th   74

The Next Door Neighbor   75

Four Houses Lost and Returned   76

Sanwa International Grocery   77

                         *

Somewhere Jazz   80

A Note of Thanks   81

Notes on the Poems   82

About the Author   85

Two Houses Down, Middle of the Night

Five quick blasts and the neighbors'
REM is quartered and drawn up under a pillow,
the horn a Morse Code to the streetlight, then somebody
leans forever on the steering wheel, a siren call
to the dead hours and whatever the hell those people
are doing now there's a voice, Billie Holiday-sleepy, opiate-toned,
drawn out in a crack-stung laugh stuck in a story
a woman is telling, there was a corner,
a bus stop, a bar no, no it's starlight clear and sluggish
not a laugh, but a sob, she's sobbing, but rageful
pissed off, honking her horn, sitting there in the front
seat in the front yard, with her fury blasting over
the flower beds and her accusations slashing at the porch where
the low panic of a man pleads *calmdown, calmdown,* but
she won't touch that because *How could you* and the horn
blasts and blasts firehouse red with the neighbors all awake as
the cop car turns the corner, lights off, jacklight searching for house numbers
as the patrolman slows and stares across the azaleas, holding
uppermost in his mind two cops, just like brothers, shot
in cold blood three months ago for a speeding ticket, less
than what this likely is, and another one murdered a year ago
just blocks from here by some nut pushing a grocery cart
with a rifle shoved under his shit, so as he passes my house, where
I'm standing on the dark front porch in my nightgown, just ear-gawking
at this mess and I point down to where it's coming from, he parks the car
away from that house, and walks with purpose but gingerly,
too, up toward the yard, calling before him, *What's up, bro?* and then
the man says, *My girlfriend's flipped out, she's all yours,* and I imagine the man
halfway backs in through the front door, because the unfairness
she's holding in her gut has turned to weeping, and the cop is talking
low and firm, helping her from the car, I think, while she weeps like a 30s starlet,
all the yelling drained out so that a muffled, moony whimper
is all that's left in the sober embarrassed knowing inside
the houses on our street which have all kept their darkness on, not one light
to put love's violence in the line-up our disapproval,
but next morning as we drive to work we see their two rocking chairs
upside down in the dirt, stuck where they landed thrown from the porch,
their curved rails sticking face up like a pair of worn scythes.

1

After the Poetry Reading, a Condom

I stepped away from the bar at Ella's where the din is handcrafted
                                    and foams up to a roar,
    as the famed poet served us his lines succulent and Southern.
With his Rhett Butler accent, the poet summoned Old Uncle Walt.
So Whitman came among us with his taste for bacony bodies
                                    and sweat-odorous men,
draped his arm over the poet and reached for the jalapeno poppers.

I stepped away from the cherry martini that had me teetering
on those heels, I hardly ever wear anymore since they kick up my bursitis,
    but I'd put in my contacts, too, so what the hell.
I stepped away from the wine-rinsed laughter and the joke I told
—if a place could have its pants down, this one does—
this mugshot of a neighborhood where I live
    with its one long avenue stretched like a nekked leg.

And what about that woman in the towel once, right there across the street,
three a.m., outfoxed by the absence of a bathtub and her mislaid name?
Of course the cops were called and they folded her like a burrito
                                    into the back seat:
    just another Tuesday night in Seminole Heights.

The night was just three beers along when I left the julep-voiced poet
    singing of Lincoln Continentals cruising the side streets,
                                    their flopping mufflers.
I walked into the after-rain on Shadowlawn Street.
Twilight sorted its lingerie in the leaves, rosy and white,
and I tottered down the block toward my car, while in all the yards,
confederate jasmine mounted the fences, bouquets on the bridal veil
                                    bushes shuddered
    and the magnolia tree came inside each mammoth blossom.

Then just as I leaned to unlock the door, I looked down at the old brick street
and saw it lying flat in the dirt, the deflated jellyfish of lust:
    used, tossed over, open-mouthed, smiling,
it was the remains of someone's poem, or at least the start of one.

The House Called Shadow Garden

Day, Inside

This crone of a house,
her cold creakiness and wind sighs.
The couch unsettles the bed. Mornings,
luck rearranges your pillow. Maybe old sorrows,
maybe bad pipes, clumsy ghosts knocking around
the front room. Once the ghost whispered in my hair,
wanted back the house. Closet doors clattered.
I threw down my dust rags, claimed every wall mine.
All afternoon, a gauzy cloud. Moss in a wet window.
Then the little porch light came on.
Later, your hands turned over the pillows,
looking for the cool side.

Night, Outside

This crone of a house,

her wind sighs and cold creakiness.
Searchlights splinter the oaks. Nights,
copters shave the roof. Maybe fireworks,
maybe gunshots, 15th Street cars riding high
on roulette wheels, the bass thumping *mothafucka*.
Windows nervous as soft teeth. Bad staggering sleep.
I thump the hot pillow, looking for the cool side.
All dark long, distant barks. The greening orange trees.
Then morning sprinklers kiss the heat.
Angel trumpet croons to walking iris:
What a pretty face you've put on.

Neighborhood Watch

When the copter roared up yesterday afternoon,
we'd just lain down into daisy light,
undone by work, drifting on a quiet acre.
Whatever it is, I murmured, *we'll see it in the paper.*

The realtor had said *up-and-coming.*
Clapboard bungalows, moss in the oaks,
old azaleas burnishing the yards.
But behind the Loma Linda, the Palm Court,
motels once wholesome as white bread,
hookers hover. Pay-Day loans and pawn shops.

This morning buried in section B:
Two Brothers Murdered by Neighbor.
Just off Idlewild and 15th.
I drive by out of lurid curiosity;
yellow tape outlines the driveway.
The house, silent as a convict.

We bought because we could afford it.
If far gunshots staple the night to dread,
happiness is a snowglobe, our house glued inside.
But above our orange-blossomed yard
the copter's a murder of buzzards.
The realtor said, *transitional.*
We're so awake it's criminal.

AT THE ROYAL PALM MOTEL

The orange sign leers over a few beat
and faded cars parked backwards to hide
the tags. A woman paces the asphalt,
walking off her jones, the voice in her
cell phone guttural, empty. A couple
limps upstairs betrothed only to bus
benches and fickle weather, while inside
#7, Robert Black still lies down
into his overdose. He's just re-read
his poem "Journey Through the Remains,"
newly published. In the jailhouse-green room
where a paint-by-number picture of an
oasis beckons towards the toilet,
he still guzzles scotch, horse gallops
through his veins. Thirty years gone.

I didn't know him then. Younger, unscathed,
I knew only what I'd heard: that he walked
like a legend of cool among vets and poets,
until his death trotted into the Royal Palm Motel
where it lingers in roach powder
and mildew. I've passed it for years. Now,
beside the open door of #7,
a man is splayed in a folding chair,
and almost drowns staring at the corner
of the parking lot where his kids splash
in their grey plastic pool. I drive by
slow and remember Robert Black. His life remains
in the little magazine that safeguards his poem,
the one that ends "find here the name my soul is."

"Please Help This Vet"

Red light at the corner of Hillsborough and Florida Avenues

His sign's propped by his VFW cap.
I'm muttering at the red light.
Clouds are grey bellies slung over the belt
of cityscape and wind swipes the street,
riffling his long grey hair, pages of his paperback.
It might be *Going After Cacciato* or *Catch 22.*
A face that battered, he may have seen Saigon that last day,
Americans swooped from the hotel roof,
copters returning like jittery swallows.

I was too young for sit-ins, the Washington march.
I drew peace signs on my cheeks, teased my hair to a 'fro.
But the first poet I knew humped Hamburger Hill,
sliced though bamboo like so many wrists.
His poems were gristled with jungle beauty.
He drank himself numb before every reading.

Here, at the light,
this vet sets back up his blown-down sign,
hunches on the curb, glasses slipping down his nose.
Should I believe the surrender of his tee?
So hard to know about folks on the street,
the broken sandals.
What if I held out a dollar?

Why do I ignore the wind-thrashed sky,
his book pages flailing as I drive on by?

OLD ORANGE AVENUE

Chubby Checker twisting them wild at Joyner's nightclub.
Ray Charles chugging down here when he played the chitlin circuit,
and before him Cab Calloway, Count Basie, Ella herself.
Even those superstars hunkered down in Jackson's Rooming House
at the edge of The Scrub, a quick shot from the train station.
It was the only place that would take them.

Tampa was a 45 record in those days
and you know who was on Side B.
Orange Avenue, the dividing line,
stretched from the Heights to downtown,
crammed with shops owned by black folks,
bright as a strip of silver tinsel.
Shop doors opened before our first coffee:
the ladies' beauty parlor, the barber's, the dress shop,
the butcher's, the vegetable man driving his truck slowly down
Lake Avenue, past Palace Drugstore into all that bustle.

But Old Jim Crow: he spread his fingers and played us all
like a minstrel tune. Made some folks crave white face
so bad they'd set a tree on fire to hear it scream.
Then the one-sided record of our life skipped, skipped, skipped;
a seethe of summers and the new interstate carved up
all the old neighborhoods, black and white. Too late.
The old avenue ignited, a blistering belt,
vinyl nights blazing like plates of gasoline.
So, city fathers erased the name, stubbed out
the flurry of daily black life. White folks sat quiet.
Flypaper hanging from the fans twisted,
twisting with black bodies in 1968.

OLD SOUTH CARRIAGE TOURS

i.
Charleston is a hot shave
when Blondie collapses in the street,
crumbling to his knees, tumbling sideways,
a thousand sacks of wet flour.
He lies for hours on cobblestones hot as andirons,
big yellow horse. Earlier, he'd been harnessed
to a wagon wide as a king-sized bed
packed with a dozen king-sized gawkers.
I'd seen him dragging that carriage,
the July furnace melting every tourist.
The driver had sing-songed the history of his city,
flicked a dozen sparks across Blondie's neck and back.
He trudged, head hanging, pulled and lugged.
As he lumbered past, I stared at his mudprints:
horseshoes plodding the wrong way,
the luck running out.

ii.
Sun flares on Saint Augustine steeples, then sinks
as I traipse a muggy side street,
slog through sticky air.
In front of Old South Carriage Tours
a stable girl hoses down a black horse,
cool water turning his coat to satin,
his mane to grosgraine tassels.
Free of harness, bridle, reins and bit,
the horse allows everything she does,
waits still as an empty urn, one on which
a muscled gelding gallops towards bronze victory,
instead of standing, head hanging,
drained muscles buckling
to chill rivulets, flicks of steam.

iii.
In swelter-dim, garage dust swirls
as Granddaddy unlocks the Impala.
I clamber over the front seat,
stare back at rusting paint cans lording over

the sooty shelves, the ruddy hood and fender.
Then we're backing out, away
from Grandmama's goldfish pond, her garden shed.
We'll just get a look-see at all the commotion, he says.

All through the Heights, the Scrubs,
before the storefronts on 7th Avenue,
Tampa is yelling breaking burning—
I'm ten. It's 1967. Folks got some strange notions.
It's decades before I'll understand how law
kept back door entrances and "Whites Only" pools,
the off-limits Walgreens counter and
all East Tampa clawing up from the gutter.
But even a child knows fair from fair.
Other times he might have brought a gun:
his Old South stunned by uppity and righteousness.
My grandfather pulls me close, tells me, *steer*,
rolls down the windows and stares.

Where Letha Lived

You know she helped raise you, says Dad.
They were lovely people.
If you went by, she always invited you in.

21st Street and 11th Avenue.
Down one end of the street a patch of tickseed
clumped around an electric substation.
Down the other end the Italians lived,
their big garden of tomatoes and greens.
The house was neat as a pin.
A pinky-beige bungalow,
faded red banister around the porch.

She and Grandmama were such good friends.
They would take a little nip of the fruitcake whiskey.
Her husband was dead.

I don't know how to feel about all this now.

*

She called our grandparents Mister and Missus.
They called her Letha.
Mondays and Tuesdays Granddaddy in his red Impala
picked her up at 8:30, took her home at 4:30.
She came in past the outdoor sinks,
past the dank garden shed,
in through the back door.

Her hands smelled of bleach. She had a gold tooth.
I believe my mother gave her our rabbit
and she made him into a stew.
Downtown it was illegal for her to eat at our table.
Her husband was dead. She had six kids.
Her children couldn't swim in our pools.

How did she feel those twenty-odd years,
walking towards the back door
on laundry Mondays, polishing Tuesdays?

How did she feel taking home our old clothes?
How did she feel hand-washing
the shorts of a Jim Crow judge?
No one ever called her the maid.

Where was her house? Puddles and mud.
A pinky-beige bungalow, red banister around the porch.
She coaxed the night-blooming cereus to light up the yard.
In the yard next door, a man looked out all day
from his green metal chair.

*

The street would have been paved, right?
Or bricks marked 1928, B'HAM ALA.
But no: mud and puddles is all I call up.
A faded bungalow, banister around the porch.
In the yard next door, a man, his green metal chair.
One end of the street, a clutch of tickseed.
The other end, the Italians, their tomatoes and greens.
She must have had a kitchen garden.
Do I remember? No.

We came in through her front door.
There was a little kitchen and a front room
where her one Navy son smiled from his frame.
Her daughters, one studying to be a nurse.
Just her and her kids. Her husband was dead.
The house was still and smelled of gardenias.
Her hands smelled of bleach.
She sat on the couch, we sat in chairs.
Cookies on a plate.
Downtown it was illegal for us to share her table.
I believe my mother gave her our rabbit and
I believe she made a stew of him.
We all called her Letha. Her calming voice.
Damn it all, I didn't know nothing at the time.

*

Damn it all, America.
Damn it all, the South.
She came in through the back door,
past the dark garden shed.
She called our grandparents Mister and Missus.
No one ever called her the maid.
No one said the N-word.
Her gardenia smell, her gold tooth.
Just her and her kids in our hand-me-down clothes.
Granddaddy in his red Impala:
8:30 to 4:30.
I don't know how to feel about all this now.
I wonder: did she own that house?
As a teen I sometimes drove her home.
I wonder: how did she feel bumping over muddy puddles,
bone–tired, the green chair man staring?

I Have Monkeys

A church-loving man, my grandfather thought Clarence Darrow
                                        betrayed us all.
Did you ever notice Darrow and Charles Darwin had the same initials?
Mr. Scopes had so intended to set the Christian world afire.

My grandfather sang deep baritone at the First Methodist.
I only noticed recently that Darrow and Darwin both begin with *d-a-r*.
Rearranged, so does *dragon*—Grand Dragon.

Remember, this was the 20's and Mr. Scopes was a man of science.
Also, my grandfather owned shotgun.
He bought stained glass and desks for the Sunday School wing.

Upstairs, at home, was a trunk where he kept the robes.
"A place for everything and everything in its place," he often said.
My grandfather knew all about high places: he was a judge.

Unlike in *The Birth of a Nation*, there were never any horses.
I learned this later when I was no longer a girl.
My grandfather was a terrific driver and it was mostly just to keep the peace.

One would drive and one would sight; the cars would troll the neighborhoods.
Somehow, *they* knew; all the homes would go silent and dark.
Divine creation meant we had never risen up from lower mammals.

The best time to scotch the snake is when it starts to wiggle.
I was grown when I first saw *Inherit the Wind*.
Mr. Scopes was a mere twenty-four and even though gasoline

can engulf a house in minutes, my grandfather always
                                        refused to see that movie.
"Evolution be damned," he said. There were never any crosses.
My grandfather sang in that church until the day he died.

Men on Bikes: A Standardized Test for White Women Alone on the Street

CIRCLE ONE:

Going to/coming from?

Backwards cap/ doo rag /black bandana

Wife beater/ hoodie /shirtless chest

Them/us/cop car

MULTIPLE CHOICE:

A. At this hour?

1. Working nightshift at Walmart
2. Might have crack in pocket
3. House robbery two blocks over
4. Eye contact/ other side of the street

B. Rider will be ticketed if he is:

1. Brown
2. Black
3. Black/Brown
4. On a bike
5. All of the above

TRUE/FALSE:

Their bikes are locked inside a cage at Sanwa Grocery, waiting for quitting time	T/F
Their bikes are locked to a metal rack at Publix, waiting for quitting time	T/F
Outside is a hose so they can get water	T/F
I gotta see their boxers	T/F
My car door is locked	T/F
I have a bike and regularly do the Sunday Ride & Ribs	T/F

CRITICAL THINKING PROBLEM:

In my mouth, bile of upstanding citizen, bile of light skin, bile of got no car, bile of do-gooder, bile of kidnap, bile of rape, bile of thug life, bile of showing your ass, bile of poverty, bile of on-edge, bile of drugs, bile of the deal, the trick, bile of handguns, bile of my vote, bile of my street, bile of knock you with a bat, bile of is, bile of seems?

SHORT ANSWER:
Pedaling with saggy pants:
Holding onto a radio:
Towing a guy on the handle bars:
Pulling a lawn mower:
Steering a second riderless bike like a show pony:

ESSAY:
Two flew past me on a street in West Tampa, sped over the cross-street without looking then flung down their bikes in front of a truck idling for the longest time at the stop sign. They thrust their heads and open hands in the driver's side window when it dropped down and that's when I knew what they were doing *(provide support)*:

SHORT ANSWER:
1. Do all poems need a generosity of spirit?
2. How do I make this stereoscopic?
3. Am I a snapshot of fear?
4. Will Somebody get mad?
5. Father-protector/mother-self, my street at twilight?

LONG ANSWER:
Whose fault is it?

Extra Credit:
First time she held you, what was your mama's dream?

LAUNDRY

We watched all night but never found out who
stole Mom's panties off the clothesline.

Before I could say what it was, I'd go in
the other bathroom and touch myself down there.

My best friend and I practiced kissing,
trading who was the man.

When Dad was out of town, Mom cooked us scrambled eggs
and hot dogs at 5pm, when she poured her first bourbon.

Burning trash, Dad caught the neighbor's punk trees on fire
and lied about it to the fireman.

Granddaddy said "colored folks" and Grandmama said "nigras."
My mother whipped us if we ever said "nigger."

The boy across the street showed me his thing
and then we didn't talk to that family for years.

All of us had ringworms.

I got my first blood on a hurricane day,
at home, in baby doll pajamas.

You Didn't Hear It from Me

My mother didn't say it, neither did Dad.
Young ladies don't talk that way.
But I did: *white trash.*

White trash called their grandmother Granny.
She carried around a tin box and spit snuff in it every 5 minutes.
White trash called their bee-hind Butt.
The white trash sister and her brothers cussed
walking home from school. *I'm gonna beat your ass!*

Their white trash mama had chipped red nails,
curlers in her hair when she shopped at Sears Roebuck.
She smoked Lucky Strikes out on the porch.
No air conditioner, one old Chevrolet.
Ketchup on eggs, bourbon on ice.
We weren't allowed to spend the night.

Friday nights at the bowling alley.
Stock car races on Saturday.
Police car in the driveway.
Their mama screaming their bloody murder names down the street.
Go get me the belt, go get the ruler,
go out to that guava bush, get me a switch.

One time the white trash girl told me, *Go get the ice.*
She iced her earlobe until it almost froze,
peered in the mirror. Pierced it with a safety pin.

That time we had a fight.
She stood by the swing set in the in-between yard
holding her mother's black butcher knife.
If you come in this yard, I'll slice you.

White trash didn't have a daddy.
Their mama sat snug to another man who picked her up
in his blue Buick because their daddy died in the war.

19

The girl shared a bike with her brothers.
She was the best at kick ball
and pricked her finger like the rest of us
and put her old doll in the shoe box
we buried to be blood sisters.

MEMORY IN GREEN

Flash at sunset I've never seen over the Gulf.
Rain trudging up from the Atlantic.
High grass in the yards on Ferris Drive and
green light of kickball games just before dusk.
Voice of the whippoorwill, the bob-white.
Putrid belly of a dead frog in the road
and the kid we blindfolded and made step in it,
we were that ugly.
Duckweed smothering the old ditch.
Live oak with the sap-green leaves
where we swayed above the bad neighbor's yard,
made up stories and practiced kissing.
Green-gold canes of the cracker roses,
lost to the yard man, the lawn boy,
and dark green whip of night-blooming cereus
that stuck itself to the magnolia tree
and flowered like New Year's Eve.
Verdigris wings of the dragonflies,
milk-green of the evening moths.
Rain like a woodblock print, horizontal
in ragged hurricane colors and the grey-green of the eye.
Flash at sunset like the luck I never spied.

FLOOD SUBJECT

Nature throwing it down,
and rain flogging the laurel oaks so they shake like drenched dogs
while light commits a drive-by at morning.

If all the frogs are gone now,
what is this hysterical glee club beyond the window
forecasting dawn and downed power lines?

Winds lashing the unmown grass,
thrashing Spanish moss out of the oaks
so that swaths strew the yard like dirty grey tee shirts.

Winds galloping down the empty avenue,
rasping the sidewalks, sandbagged and abandoned,
as the day flips inside out like a cheap umbrella.

New band of surges, and, for godsakes,
what is the true subject toppling the sunflowers,
the one that won't recede no matter how clear the outlook?

Same old report:
loss, loss, a station I can't seem to change.

DANNY JACKSON MUST NOT DIE

Bowers House, Canon, Ga.

He plucked that child from
the machinery of the afterlife.

We were on the upstairs
porch at the writer's house.
It was still a living house.
Set back so deep in magnolia dim,
homefolks barely knew it was there.

The night was like bootblack
when Greg drove up.
A black sedan trailed him
around mixed-up blocks,
Dixie flag on the license plate.
But the week was pre-paid.
He shut himself up in the ivy room
and wrote and wrote.
Jeff took the aging vanity,
Michael, the corner porch swing,
MJ spread out on the dusty couch.
We all wrote and wrote.

Way back in Georgia farm country,
a busted little town.
They'd ditched the brick factory,
deserted the crumbling church.
The forsaken stores on Main Street:
piles of broken mannequins,
rat-chewed candy bars.
Under the awnings,
swallows nested in the eaves.

Everyone asks:
Aren't there ghosts?
Antique bedposts,
rusted anvil in the cellar.
Names of the family scratched
in the attic beams.

The woman in the cloche and
the boy with the toy plane got old,
then they rented rooms
to the cotton merchants—
9   10   11
on the doors.
At night a clanging of gears,
a jittery clatter.
Someone moving the furniture.
It's just the train clanking
the old cotton-shipping tracks,
rails so close they rim the azaleas.

I set a fan, a rocker, and a table
on the upstairs porch, thought,
if I stayed in this rocker
all summer long,
I'd still never match
the heroics of that boy.

West Bowersville, twilight,
rum, screech owl in magnolia leaves,
lone boy out on his bike,
a place for old freight trains.
The stories barreled down
about men like Danny Jackson:

He was just a kid himself
and the Ford veered into his own bones.
Crushed his jaw, but he survived;
middle-aged by now.

I'll never forget:
it was empty as a birdbath, his mouth.

Night Train and Little Owl

When you hear the tone, the time will be dreaming,
says her voice, little slide down a thumb piano.

Night train skirting 30th Street warns the restless cars of East Tampa,
Stay back, I'm hauling the moon.

Little owl resumes her night-sky cantata, her voice skimming
octaves like fingernails on the teeth of a comb.

Night train screeches out short and long O's
to urge her on to deeper mysteries,

the curiosities of street lamps, the vagaries of raccoons.
They pass their voices back and forth until

all the coupled cars trace the edge of the city.
Blocks away, stock boys unload oranges at Sanwa Grocery,

young teachers plump their pillows, newly-minted 4th graders wrestle
first-day-of-school nightmares, while somewhere in the unlit yard

a paisley voice smelling of mole crickets and young jays
practices her scales up and down the registers of the mulberry tree.

The train responds with thunka thunka, carrying its cargo of graffiti,
hooting awake the crossing guards, the heavy-eyed sun, the tuneless stars.

Where Shopping is a Pleasure

Publix Supermarket, Nebraska Avenue, Tampa

Saturday nights we rush the outside ATM
while our ride waits in the fire lane
under the riled gaze of the security guard.

The old security guard:
limping with bursitis,
grey-haired, black, unarmed,
how could she secure anything?
Now there's this man, white,
young, gun snug at his belt.

Sundays, we bulge the checkout lines
when they start selling beer.
We swoop down the wine aisles
in scuffed heels, work boots,
maybe bedroom slippers.
We're tailgaters in a chicken wing frenzy,
church ladies in sherbet-colored hats.

Wanna Lotto?
At the Service Desk we line up nine deep.

Did you find everything you need?
Do they really want to know
if we found that house we could afford,
the one with the porch so spacious and blue?
Or what about that City job,
the one we might sail on for years?

Fresh salmon might be what we need,
but farmed catfish is BOGO.
We find comfort in lemon-lime soda and Fritos.

Did you find everything you need?
Plant City strawberries snag us with scent,
taking us back to when shortcake was a given.
We trudge out the double doors

wondering about an answer.
Hard to say.
                    An empty plastic bag
claims the one free space in the parking lot
and the security guard is headed our way.
He's been shooing us off for hours.

Professional Development: Active Shooter
Because these days you never know.

Visually scan the venue.
Identify possible exits.
Work to build a barricade.
This is what it's come to.

Today I am earning 3 credits
in a place of higher learning.
Is there anywhere to hide?
Police Chief: *gotta face it.*

One brother has his many many.
One brother has his big big.
At home I've got zilch.
I'm afraid to be that deadly.

Dad's weapons when we were kids:
Just a bunch of wooden clubs.
He'd served during the war.
Maybe he'd shot enough.

Next session up: explosives.
Head of Security: twitchy.
Later I enter the classroom of freshmen.
Every backpack's loaded.

HEADLINE: Student had Gun, Cops Say

Latin King, strutting
your bad walk, strolling
in late, flashing
the hand talk your boys
require, the cramped, crossed
fingers and flared palms,
I sit you up
front, near me, for the work
you never do, your folder
as a point of pride packing
only those odd syllables
and signs that I don't get. Even
here under the teacher's nose
you ink over
and over the three-point
crowns that crowd the kingdom
of your notebook. Once
I found you holding court
for your classmates, curious
innocents, struck by
the hieroglyphs of your black
bandana. Soon after, I would
shudder with the weight
of what you packed
through the halls that day
you didn't get to class. The last
time you left my room, we
watched you strap on
cockiness, fingering the taboo
smokes in your pocket.
At the bell
you adjusted your slick
black locks and swaggered
out, then down dark
halls to your chosen realm.

POLITICS

When the blue jays suddenly caucus
in the aisles of a summer afternoon,
screaming of a cabal,
I rush to raise up the window in our bathroom,
thinking to witness calamity.
My cat leaps onto the sill, toting his indoor wistfulness,
and together we peer towards the deserted yard
of the bad next-door neighbor.

The guttural feral cat is batting something in the grass.
She turns her dark mottled head to us:
her nose is pale as a tombstone.
The cardinals picket in the dead orange tree,
crying their dissent—*pip, pip, pip!*
and the whole yard is simultaneously frantic:
the squirrel ranting from the fencepost and
the filibustering mockingbirds in
low branches of the live oak.
Even the terra cotta rabbit seems to shriek of a red alert,
even the zebra butterfly trembling in the dill.
My cat sniffs hard and quick.

Only the ceramic angel is uninvolved:
slumped among the four o'clocks,
she stares mutely at her broken feet.

Balancing, Truing, and Personal Service

This evening the first perfume of confederate jasmine
    is preparing to set us right
        as the moon lifts and loosens
the buds with her curved white wrench
and they hum
    an idling song,
        ivory and green,
    while all night the street sounds lurch over them,
the thunderous mufflers, the bed-shaking bass,
    the sirens screeching up the highway
        to their frightened breathless scenes
        and all night
                inside a springtime thrum
    as in an ode to the great wheel,
the song veers over our flat sleeping streets
    and jasmine hums along all the fences
unmuffled and steady,
    and the song is one ode to the big rotation,
        the harmony asking without wobble or shudder,
What world do you want?
    And will you wake,
        amidst the moony drone, the fragrant purring, the pumping streets,
will you wake and drive your life into the answer?

after Mary Oliver

The Ember of the Nursing Home

The cigarette butt in the nursing home parking lot
is cold as metal on the lift Jorge swings out
every morning to weigh Mrs. McAllister,
a small loaf of bread in the sling.

    Jorge, who every Tuesday and Friday
bathes Mr. Romero, his Purple Heart,
Mr. Hall, his going kidneys,
with the tenderness of an *abuela*,
his own lost now to the bad sugar.

    He changed her bedclothes himself,
rolling her from one safety rail to the other
so she hardly knew the dank sheets were whisked away,
fresh ones stretched snug below her.

    Jorge lugs down the hall the loaded linen cart
heaped with musty towels, the pillow cases
they use in this place, stained mattress covers,
grim bedspreads smelling of armpits and toes.

    Jorge, who bears on his arm Mr. Allen, needing again
the toilet since cancer claimed his prostate.

    Jorge, who in one sure hedge against falls
during her 6 AM perambulations,
clutches the safety belt of Miss Washington
even though she gives him the evil eye
like his sixth grade teacher who thought he was cheating.

    His shoulders are thick as two *lechon*.

    Jorge, who spends lunchtime in his car:
reggaton, Cuban sandwich, Red Bull.

    Jorge, one amber wave in a thousand,
little ember of Boricua.

    Jorge, who heads into the afternoon shift,
his lips until the last second close around his cigarette
like two fingers encircling a wrist or
a sea surrounding an island.

Nebraska Avenue Torch Song

Don't be a downer, Buy your partner some flowers
sign on the street

From Body Parts of America to Mercy Church,
the white plaster cat on the funeral home roof
has seen it all. 15 miles of *wish-you-were-here:*
Nebraska Avenue, first gateway to Tampa,
sweet times on the river and a plunge in Sulphur Springs.
Nebraska Avenue, glory of the 20s.

    But tin-can tourists left before we were born.
    The high flume ride was scrapped for Alpine Liquors.
    The fancy arcade made way for a dog track.

Since then, the white plaster cat's been our eyewitness
to unrequited lives flopping in the sheets of old motels—
Casa Loma, Loma Linda, Swan Oasis and Royal Palm.
Recovering addicts in the halfway house.
Sidewalks crammed with sofas, stoves, the furniture of moving-on,
the jilted, neglected, deserted and dumped.

Let's turn down this bed.

The river and springs are still alive.
Young neighbors are planting azaleas.
On her slope above the scenery,
the white plaster cat is holding fast.
Last time they remodeled the funeral home,
they shingled a new roof and ditched the white cat.

    But they had to put her back.
    The people were in love.

Winter Solstice, Paris Street
21 December 2012

Tonight my friend of thirty years
hobbles up the walkway at the end of the 4th world,
her dreadlocks decades-long, perfumed with patchouli.
The morning paper lies in the yard like a bludgeoned fish.

In the long count on the shortest day, we start our letting go.
Holding slender candles, we anoint ourselves with rosemary, bay oil,
lay out our griefs and losses, first one then the other, like solitaire.
We consider the end of the Mayan Calendar,
the three failed worlds that came before.

I think, *Do we believe in anything anymore?*
So we snuff the candles and sit unspeaking in the ruffled dark.
Spanish moss unfolds its silver pashminas and
the long night wends itself through the garden.
In the empty pit, I coax up a fire from newspaper, fallen oak.

The grey cat we call Lucky, the cat no one wanted,
nuzzles our feet and we're bathed in the greeny air, the woodsmoke.
All down our block, wind chimes sound in the breeze
before rain like temple bells.
My friend rocks in her seat, remembering poems.
Next year's door creaks open.

A dozen gilt moons glow in the orange tree.
Silent as a gong, the real moon peers down, gleams.

EXAMINING THE CANNON

Tampa Bay Hotel, 1898

How gingerly they rest their hands on its barrel,
the solid heft of it.
How familiar they seem in its presence,
like crowding around an old patriarch.
One fellow with the look of a soldier
slouches beside it easily as lounging in the sun.
He savors his cigarette, daydreams about rain.
One gent in a black suit and bowler makes notes in a little book,
staring down into the death maw as if it were a wishing well.
One man in summer-white linen and straw hat strokes it there,
on the worn fire-mouth, powder-soft O of fury.

Blocks away, in our dank shuttered houses,
we iron our restlessness,
darning their socks, sewing buttons to their uniforms.
After tea-cakes, after shutting the lamps,
we will bid our husbands good night
and herd the giddy anxieties of war that we,
the weaker sex, are prone to back onto the fainting couch.
We will say our prayers to Almighty God
and ask for an end to strife,
and try not to hope for more,
since women are nothing
in the face of men and their fascinations.

36

Pecha Kucha for Big Guava

[Hillsborough River, 1920]

Back when we counted all the animals on the banks:
snapping turtle, hoot owl, anhinga, little possum.
Otters swam their rap, manatees drifted in river jazz.
What can you say of home?—Just press on it, a good hurt,
    press on it over and over.

[Confederate monument on grounds of county courthouse, 1921]

In Court House Square they sang Dixie
and cheered. The marble rebels stood guard,
staring down black folks hoping for fair trials.
We always knew why it was put there.
As if, justice, really, were part of the Lost Cause.

[Spectators on Lafayette Street Bridge watching invasion of Gasparilla ship, 1922]

There was no Jose Gaspar, no pirate island,
but who wouldn't want to think so?
Our doctors, lawyers, brokers, and bankers sailed
into the century on a motley ship, christened themselves mystic.
We're still lapping up their drunken revelry.

[Bungalow, 5610 Branch Ave., 1922]

She's standing there like a ghost, but really
it was her house first. Those cabbage palms,
bougainvillea, white gardenia, beauty bush.
Her crone of a house wreathed in cracker rose. Now:
sandspurs, boarded up windows, a locked door.

[Sulphur Springs Pool, swimmer exiting toboggan ride
watched by crowd on bridge, 1922]

We crowded the heights and thrilled
second-hand to the slips, squeals and splashy falls
of the most courageous. Until 1929: the whole
country goes free-fall like a busted toboggan.
Everyone loves a plummet.

[Klan Rally, Lakeland, 1923]

The front row woman trounced up and rushed the hostess.
I'm sick, she said, *of white people saying white people
are bad.* I'd just read *The night was like bootblack.*
My father was Italian: he never forgot the sign at our lake.
This was 1950: *No Coloreds, No Daigos, No Dogs.*

[Plant Park, 1923]

Gasparilla queens and cigar magnates' wives.
Confederate jasmine, pastel bonnets.
The riverside park now mocks sea wall graffiti,
blooms in downtown's neon. Magnolia dream:
men and their closed clubs, mere coins in our pond.

[Lake Roberta, 1925]

Used to be, she was the city's looking glass
when rain was good and stringers were full of trout.
These twilights, we have our little promenade.
Trucks still pull over for hookers, but at Christmas
she's ringed with lights and Santa's sleigh floats.

[Street scene Bayshore Boulevard at DeSoto Avenue looking south, 1925]

First, it was just crushed shell snaking through palmetto.
Now: The world's longest sidewalk.
Weekends, we make it our own. We run and pedal
towards sundown, the brine of Hillsborough Bay
urging us faster towards whatever's everlasting.

[Tampa Bay Hotel, keyhole opening, 1926]

Outside the keyhole, Southern splendor lurches
toward heatstroke. Here, elf-light and guilding,
big mirror on the landing. So many jobs for new Americans:
Italians made bricks, Irish made beds. A German hunting guide
led you to your kills—now his family are plumbers.

[Seventh Avenue, Ybor City, 1927]

The Hatchet Judge, they called my grandfather: swinging
at Ybor speakeasy doors, making sure it was all in the movies.
Bolita was the game. Everybody was on the take. Blocks away
my future family was dressing corpses, making hooch.
Wild Ybor City, where did you slink off to?

[The Tampa Bay Hotel, 1929]

A poem in latticework and brick: The winter hotel's long-defunct.
A man says the halls hold disembodied laughter.
A lady in Victorian dress is another rumor.
Six crescent moons, six minarets.
Alone, I feel my arm hairs perk up.

[Bayshore, 1930]

The bay smells like must, pelicans, old hope.
Once we saw manatees beneath Davis Islands Bridge.
Remember? Mr. Davis flat out disappeared way back in the 20s.
He left behind his bougainvillea neighborhood.
The world's longest sidewalk like the shadow of his smile.

[Tampa Theatre, 1931]

The organist at her keyboard rises up from below stage.
Mae West, Josephine Baker. Stars pinprick the ceiling.
Once black folks could sit only in the balcony.
Now the theatre's crowded with hipsters, old academics,
a stuffed peacock. A stairwell of empty reels.

[Cigar Workers, 1935]

When Tampa abandoned her corset,
cigar rollers still raised children, still rubbed their chapped hands.
By the front door of their *casitas*, fresh Cuban bread hung on a nail.
Now Ybor's full of baristas and barmaids,
boutique olive oil as lush as payday.

[Orange picking scene at Stebbins Grove, 1936]

What we have now: orange trees
in the throes of citrus greening. A ladder-fall
could cripple you and the boundless haul killed
your shoulders. But even when the boss man just watched,
the fruit was gorgeous in your palm.

[Farm Workers in Celery Field, 1945]

I won't get into it, but there were lynchings.
Everyone knows it who wants to know. So let's move on
to the celery farms. They were right there in Gary,
east of Ybor City. The old postcards show everything.
Celery and cigars. We had to be famous for something.

[Traffic in front of Sulphur Springs Arcade at 8100 Nebraska Avenue, 1946]

Springs lured the sick to their healing
waters and tourists to the spa-like arcade.
Lemonade in the lobby, foxtrots in the dance hall.
By the 70's, we could skate the vacant walkway.
Then it all got bulldozed for progress, a dog track.

[Gasparilla, Franklin Street, 1953]

From the window of Granddaddy's office,
I swear we saw a pirate get run over—
one cousin firing his cap gun, one in an eyepatch.
The building's gone, the beads are fake. I won't lift my shirt
to show my boobs. But I scream like a banshee, *Beads! Beads!*

[Sulphur Springs, 1954]

Uplighting, bats, and who's going to save it. Sometimes
vets in motorized chairs rest at the base, rearrange their flags.
Sometimes there's a concert, sometimes movie night.
The tower sings copters and wind-thrashed sky.
When new bridges turn neon, the tower's just old
    and the brown river, striped.

NEW YEAR'S EVE, PARIS STREET
31 December 2016

It's a new America and next year's door's propped open.
Already somebody's shooting a gun, though we all know
falling bullets have to lodge somewhere.

No, it's the same old, just a shitload of fireworks
trucked in from South of the Border.
The neighbors signed the forms, etcetera.
They'll be up all night rocking the block,
scaring the veterans.

Somebody says, *I don't believe in anything anymore.*
Someone else is planning to protest.
Someone saves for a march that will really count.

Somehow, a dozen gilt moons peer from the orange trees.
The real moon reaches crescendo.

We toss back our cheap champagne.
We count to ten and start our letting go.

THE GOOD SAMARITAN OF FLORIDA AVENUE

The long hall of sleeping orphans dims in the 1960s.
My father brought us along past the Christmas lights.
Our bundles held outgrown picture-day dresses, Easter shoes.
Poor little things, said my mother.
Later The Children's Home closed,
the orphans shipped out to the country.

    tulip tree   jacaranda   crepe myrtle   oleander

When the old Floridan Hotel was a flophouse,
my friend played his saxophone out the window.
Way before that, it was all glamour.
My mother sang "Blue Moon" in the Sapphire Lounge.

    Lucky's Shamrock   *The Golden Anchor*

All night long at Faedo's Bakery men roll loaves
of Cuban bread, turnovers full of guava paste.
You'll buy some and think of your granny or *nonna*,
grandma or *abuela* when the sign says HOT.

    Make You Happy Food Mart

In the yard of The Good Samaritan, the old Children's Home,
Ed passes time in a folding chair.
Ed, his all night pain and bad teeth.
Ed, who plumbed all the schools till his back went.
Then he got hired to greet tourists where I worked.
Ex-Army, friendly as a puppy.

    Gladys Street   Flora Vista   Fortune Street   Orange Blossom

Joe Haskins has fixed our bikes forever.
His hands are cramped, but young black men
and Mexican pickers bring him their broken wheels.
There's a hose out front so they can drink.

    Homeless helping Homeless   *Hope is Here*

A man rushed the huge doors at Sacred Heart Church.
Give me a sign of your goodness. They were locked.
He dropped to his knees, crossed himself, started praying—
desperation manifest on Florida Avenue.

Faith Walkers Worldwide   Divinity Inspections

The long hall of The Good Samaritan lists into 2017.
Ed and the other working poor line up for the moldy bathroom.
Once our pretty boss lady said, *Get your scented candles.*
Round up your handmade soaps and homemade marzipan.
We'll all do it, she said, *to make him basket.*
And so she got out of Ed's Christmas bonus.

Lord have mercy on us all

In Sumptuous Ticking

Boyd's Clocks, Tampa

There's no tinkle to the door.
In the dwindling aisles, no one.
But a voice calls: *Back here.*
He's antique himself, slight as a pre-teen,
his electric wheelchair massive.
Hair, threadlike. Teeth and smile, still his.
I'm agog with ding-dongs and pendulums.
My grandmother's Seth Thomas in my arms,
I've come to the last living clock shop in Tampa
for a *Set-Wind-Clean.*

I set my grandmother's bequest
on a smidgeon of desk. Rustled chimes jingle
amidst tocking and dim.
He starts spinning back Tampa-time,
old connections engaging gears:
my father, his teacher after the war,
taught him to speak in front of strangers.
He calls up scraps of speeches, stories,
the classmate from Plant City who
for three weeks worked up courage just to say his name.
The pen and pencil set, his prize for most improved.

Another dong-ding and I remember why I've come.
Together we admire the four cherubs on her face,
the symmetry of her wedding-ring dial.
A fine patina of the 30s is gathered in the grooves.
We find the missing winding key
wedged in a corner behind the works,
study the scribbled record of old cleanings,
handle the brittle electric cord—*yes, original.*
Then he tells the story of the great flood
that drowned all the minutes in the Seth Thomas factory.
It's a pretty fine clock, he says,
his hands rubbing the case,
the familiar perpetual motion.

My father is 90.
In not too long a time he'll be dead;
so will Mr. Boyd; so will I.
Onyx mantel clocks, lazy camelbacks,
brass-handled carriage clocks, neon alarms,
the cuckoos with their dancing peasants,
lyre clocks with poem-like bells,
longcases standing sentry like grandparents
peering out for the past-curfew:
soon they'll all need repair and I will be back
in my grandmother's parlor,
listening to chimes, their judicious knelling.

STILL LIFE
on the ground beside the porch

As if a gray sock were filled with sand
As if a long twist of yarn unraveled itself
And stretched out in the dirt
As if the snug pile of chopped maple were a nest
As if green bottleflies confused their two ways
As if one pomegranate seed were lost to dust
As if four miniature hands were reaching
with delicate nails clawing for sun,
As if stagger could zigzag across our porch
As if inevitable could be animal vegetable mineral
As if a wisp of god snuggled in the possum baby brain
As if this all could be taken back from rain.

In the Midst of Magnolia

Your stories buried in the blooms, the creamy bowls of magnolia
we brought in from your yard to fill your kitchen with a woozy piquance.

The fading house on Rainbow Road
where voices ping-ponged in your brain.

Your odd magic wrestled from a typewriter, a glass of wine.
A phrase slugged out between drugs and cigarettes.

The black and white that hung over your desk where you sat framed
in white wicker. Your child perched on the arm like an awkward pet.

Palm fronds, frog song, a flashback on the page.
Black-eyed susans and an orange grove.

A raunchy clause where the sexy you stretched herself out.
The corner of purple and blue, your bedroom bullseye.

                    The poem I wanted for you has failed me. Here:

On long drives out to your house stars made a cliché of sky.
There was a gateway from grief and you walked through it.

                    Magnolia perfume is the gist of it.

for Joelle Renee Ashley

Sorry About that Thing I Heard

These are not the three-day wakes of Brooklyn,
the black-Old-World-clothes, crawl-on-your-knees,
Don't-leave-me-mama! wakes.

These are the night-long family visitations of the South,
pews stuffed with perfumed great-aunts, their rosaries,
the heaving red-eyed uncles. This is where the blonde turns
aside from the mourning crowd to observe, *They all look like Mafia.*

*

This is the West Tampa funeral of the last bolita-runner with no one
but his handy man to stand up and declare, *He treated me right.*

Here is the seven-hour Home-going for the young secretary,
the August all-day in the un-air-conditioned A.M.E. church.
Her baby girl and little man squirming next to Granma,
the praying and fanning, singing and moaning.
After three hours I couldn't take it no more.

*

When Letha died, so many years after the end
of her work-morning knocks at Grandmama's back door,
her laundry days steeped in bleach, her ruined hands
polishing the good silver, her tongue running over her gold tooth,
when she died even though none of us had seen her in years,
except to drop off a Christmas ham,
we all went together to the A.M.E. church
and cried for the long gone times.
Her daughter had our names in the program
and made us sit up front with family.

*

When my student's brother got killed
we brought her mama the school collection,
over five-hundred dollars, and she worried about how
I'd get to the service in that part town I didn't know,
deciding right then, I'd ride in the black car with her and the kids.

*

I remember Nannù's family: Ybor City funeral parlor,
Prohibition, jugs of hooch hauled in the back of their hearse.
Years later, Joey picked up a girl in the big black car
while a cigar maker's body stiffened in the back.

Across town on my Southern side:
Mom's undertaker uncle,
his two-room funeral home tacked to the rear of his house,
no alcohol for a mile, his cousin-in-law begging us
never to have her viewing there after she heard him
tell pallbearers loading a coffin, *Slide him right on in.*

American Pantoum

We're hurting. Words reach for healing.
I'm constrained in terms of talking about the details.
There were candles. There were signs.
The scattering of light might have caused it.

I'm constrained in terms of talking about the details,
but at some point, we all have to reckon with this.
A scattering of light might cause it.
There are, of course, a tangle of factors.

At some point, we all have to reckon with it.
A sense of grievance. It's our culture.
There are, of course, a tangle of factors,
like the colors preceding a storm.

It's our culture. A sense of grievance.
It doesn't happen in other places with this kind of frequency.
There are theories about the color preceding a storm.
Publicly toting guns amps up the danger.

It doesn't happen in other places with this kind of frequency.
All I know is this must stop. This divisiveness.
Publicly toting guns amps up the danger.
I had to take a pretty big breath to get that out.

All I know is this must stop. This divisiveness.
When will enough people say, Stop this madness?
I took a pretty deep gulp. My voice was shaking.
Someone had no trouble getting his hands on a gun.

When will enough people say, Stop this madness?
Taking one or two lives at a time, all the time,
someone had no trouble getting his hands on a gun.
The chairs were left empty for the men killed.

Taking one or two lives at a time, all the time:
craven politicians and the NRA.
The chairs were left empty for the men killed.
In the middle of a firefight, it's hard to pick out the good guys.

Craven politicians and the NRA.
We should say to ourselves, Not one more.
In the middle of a firefight, it's hard to pick out the good guys.
There is something particularly heartbreaking about it.

We should say to ourselves, Not one more.
But I've seen how inadequate words can be;
There is something particularly heartbreaking about it.
Police say the shooter also died.

I've seen how inadequate words can be.
We don't leave it up to officers to work solo.
We have not 20, but 50 casualties.
Try picturing mountains in the distance.

We don't leave it up to them to work solo.
There were candles, there were signs,
mountains in the distance, the deepening blue.
We don't have to live like this.

I had to take a pretty big breath to get this out.

DID YOU FIND EVERYTHING YOU NEED?

Publix Supermarket, Nebraska Avenue, Tampa, March 22, 2016

I'd just heard on the car radio about Brussels.
I pull through the dry cleaners horror-dazed,
my chore list slumped in the seat.

What's the use of poetry? How can it matter now?
I thought, *One more quick stop and I'm just going home.*

At Publix, sans cart or basket, I zoom down
Aisle 6, Paper Products, claw down
two jumbo paper towel rolls, zip
around the corner towards 7, Pet Food, and almost
collide. He stands rooted before the wood
cleaners—his dreads blond-black, his red hoodie
unzipped, his right calf a full cuff of bruise-blue
tats. I dash towards Canned Cat Food.
Shreds versus Filets, ten for six dollars.
I'm stacking two, three, four,
five cans on my right palm
with jumbo rolls jammed
in my elbow crease, teetering, tenuous,
when a burnt-match smell
edges in from the right. He's a grainy image
stopping behind my left shoulder. I concentrate on
Dry Food and don't turn round.

Would you like this?
He removes pine cleaner, quinoa, bottles of juice.
Sets down his basket.
It's okay, I'm heading towards checkout just now.
No, but so am I.
Arms loaded, he's already walking off as I yell,
Thanks! You did your good deed for the day!
He slows, calls back over his shoulder,
I hope that's not all. There's still a lot of day left.

59

THANKSGIVING EVE AT FAMILY DOLLAR

Nebraska Avenue, Tampa

My lucky day off, Thanksgiving Eve is August-hot.
Hitchcock & Sons is hand-painting
the white fence of Family Dollar.
Tar in the truck cauldron roils.
Mulch in the wheelbarrow steams.
One son in unlaced boots makes
the white outlines of parking spaces pristine.
One son lays sod along the edge of the lot.
In the shade, their three little kids
draw cartoons on the new blacktop.

What's it like to be Hitchcock & Sons?
I don't have to pull a brush across a fence.
But my worries pile up like dirty spoons.
Maybe Hitchcock & Sons are finally out of debt,
their big family driving in.

Once my son found a hundred dollar bill right there.
At home, my mom's platters and silver.
I want something polished for Hitchcock & Sons.
I want something polished for myself.
I back out, cheap drip pans and tin foil rustling,
two bags of ice melting towards Thanksgiving.

From Sea to Shining

O beautiful, for the seats in the rental car are spacious
and wanderlust winks in the moonless skies.
It's the day before the 4th of July.
We've been stuck in our workweeks like bees in amber;
even the Gulf with its kitten-cat waves can't free us.
The grain of the dashboard gleams as we pack the car
in the purple, pre-dawn light. The highway hums
its serenade, old song of the open, etcetera.

We're bound for mountains with just an old school Triptik;
bound for the majesty of grazing cows,
the Eastern bluebird, the rhododendrons,
and once past Atlanta, fruited with drivers illegally texting,
we can just plain breathe.

Up along HWY 441, we feel our bodies returning.
You can still recognize God's America, even
with the new WalMart glowing on the hill and KFC in the valley.
God himself must have shed every expectation,
so when we make the turn onto Coweeta Church Road

and finally hear the grace-notes of cicadas
and see the mountains crowned with rain
and know the fireworks will be spoiled tomorrow,
even so, we think it is good.

The car bounces up the mountain until we park
at the house poised on the very peak. Here,
let us join the brotherhood of dropouts for the long holiday weekend.
Fugitives from a sea of purposes and connections,
let us fix our eyes on the purple mountains,
let us gaze on nothing but you, Oh Beautiful.

FAIRYLAND

Lowry Park, Tampa, 1960s

Of course there was a rainbow.
Pixie paths looped beneath live oak and everybody there was stuck in *Freeze!*
Humpty Dumpty, the King, Rapunzel singing from her safe-house.
The Magic Dragon roller coaster tracked our fate in clouds.

The Jolly-Good-Fellow my dad took us there on Saturdays.
My mom was in bed with her left-behind dreams.

On car trips, my mother would sing *two little clouds bumped their heads*
    and claim before this life, she'd lived with fairies.
But they'd cast her out and now she was our mother.

When little clouds cried, fairies wiped the tears,
then hung their gowns on sunbeams: *indigo, violet, aquamarine.*
    In her late-morning bed, my mother flew to the edges of her room.
Her bedsheets fluttered in a peacock mist.

Where are you? asks Tinkerbell.
In the whale whose mouth you walk into, at the pond freckled with pennies.
    Back at the swings, we pumped our legs towards bliss.

BOUTONNIERE

In the blue bathroom, my mother's hidden Kotex.
My pajama crotch smeared with first blurred fire.

Hard to describe the side yard: dog chain,
verbena, teens bristling in collars of restless fire.

Slow dancing with vertigo in my home-made gown.
I catch the room careening through satin skull-fire.

Grey-tone, the old Polaroid. My father's car keys: sweaty.
My big-girl mouth blotted with *Ring of Fire*.

Late radio singing "Sunday Morning Coming Down."
If women are guitars, here's a strummed, plucked fire.

Dead, the boy whose fingers slaked my breasts.
You'd recognize the name: smudge of swallowed fire.

REVEREND BILLY'S BOOGIE WOOGIE
AND MOM'S GULBRANSEN
The Palladium Theatre, Saint Petersburg, FL.

We're here for the Hillbilly Deathmatch.
Two balladeers duking it out:
heartbreak vs. boogie woogie,
Les Paul guitar vs. Steinway Baby Grand.
The Friday Night music palace seeps age and glory—
rows of faded velvet seats, wooden backs worn smooth
from decades of sweat and delight.

The balladeer's got the guitar: his fingerwork is a cheery stroll,
his second-tenor-muttered lyrics walking us around the yard,
down the block to the intersection of Heartbroke and Wanting More.
We're referees: our seat-shifting and half-yawns call it:
no way is that round going to him.

Then Reverend Billy stomps on stage
in a cowboy zoot suit and kickass boots.
He pounces on the ivories, his hands
the tarantella, the electric slide, the St. Vitus dance of boogie woogie.
We hoot and jive in our seats.
It's a musical K.O.

God, it feels good to get shaken this way,
after months of putting the house to sleep,
forcing a coma on one room at a time.
Rev says he wants to slow it down, *play somethin pretty.*
Melodic and melancholy, it takes me
to my mother's back room
where her old upright Gulbransen sags unsold, untuned.
She filled the house with show tunes and old standards—
South Pacific, Annie Get Your Gun, her low alto tremolo.
It's been mute for years.

Rev caresses the Steinway.
Behind him the velvet curtains are crenelated, ballooned.
Above him the stage lights are blue as my mother's eyes.

THE METHODIST WOMEN'S SOCIETY COOKBOOK

United Methodist Church, Ybor City, circa 1953

Make me a saint by getting meals and washing up the plates.

The recipe pages crumble fine as confectioner's sugar:
  Cold Relish and *Egg Delight, Scripture Cake, Yankee Doodle Pie.*
The fellowship of *Eight in One Casserole.*

Mix lightly

My grandmother's church: every Mother's Day,
the ladies of The Women's Society wore corsages like fluffy divinity.

Divide into two parts

Is it still a church? Across the street is a used car lot.
Next door, a trashed bungalow.

Let stand two or three hours

Miles south, in a parking lot, people wait in the lattice of fading sun.
November till March, they lump together:
the addicts, the homeless, the curdled minds.

A good light dinner when cold

In the alley near the convention center, the swatch of grass under the bridge,
they wait for a heap of meatloaf. Wait for a slab of turkey.
There aren't *guava shells, nutmeats, pickled rind* or *orange ring.*

Save a small amount

The new website of the old church says it isn't a church. Just some folks
serving their ministry. Friday lunch and dinner in the social hall.
Followed by Bible study. Followed by ambrosia.

Prevent them from sinking to the bottom.

Online, last year's photos: ladies in the kitchen, men crowding a table,
a young mother and her girls in pink: empty plates, lemon-pie grins.

It will all be much easier to handle.

What does it take to do good in this world?
The Women's Society, their hats of chiffon.

Write extra recipes here.

Best Supporting Role
Fun-Lan Drive In, Hillsborough Ave. and 22nd Street, Tampa, 1960s

Next to 22nd Street, the shell lot is stuck to the railroad track. The night magic of our youth hunkers in dust.

Fun-Lan Drive-In: speakers hang like charms from the windows of the Ford Fairlane. One majestic screen opens onto summer's first night. Up front, Dad and Mom are Saluting the Civil War Centennial in Technicolor: *Gone With The Wind* bustin' out the bar-b-que and fiddle-dee-dee. Dad's crunching potato chips. Mom sucks a black olive, then a Pall Mall, blows smoke towards the flare of the concession stand. In the back seat, watching Mammy cinch Scarlett's waist so tight, my sisters and I stuff our faces with pimento cheese, corn chips and Coke. We're planning which swings to grab at intermission when Mom's *shush*ing wafts back towards us. As Gallantry Takes a Last Bow, she's already breaking down the old rules. Hattie McDaniel was the first African American to win the Academy Award. But we kids don't know a thing about that, just that Mom's started a new job at Head Start, she's made her first Negro friend and next weekend the NAACP folks are coming for dinner.

BETWEEN MICKEY MOUSE
AND I DON'T GIVE A DAMN
Confederate flag, I-4, between Tampa and Orlando

Frankly, my dears,
it's giving us the finger.

Big as a battlefield this red X blue salutes commuters.
Rebel ghosts prowl the fields lining I-4
in search of the venerable Past.
Disney shimmers in the distance like a magic salve.

So this is Dixie, where white gloves
parasol into white hoods and this damn flag
flutters like a cartoon flip-book.
Somebody's wet-dream of heritage.

Yes, I had a great-grandad
and he come from Alabam, but
this X marking the spot is a tumble
into Fantasia: Mickey's red cape, his blue sorcerer's hat,
all our white skin.

To hell with our ♫ *Way down upon* ♪.
I want to worship at the church of setting right.
I want a flood of sanctified song,
unsung as the Suwannee herself:

                      free-flowing, tannic dark, and righteous as sweet oil.

CORNER OF BLANCO AND SOUTH STREETS
Saint Augustine, FL

A collapsing shack loiters at the sidewalk's edge
just a hairsbreath from the blue cottage we're renting,
little cottage that's letting us breathe for a few days,
tucked away from our real lives.
Falling out somebody's yard, shell-stone and coquina.
Peculiar as an outhouse in this grand oak neighborhood.
I've got to find it out.
Boarded window holes, boarded doors, but what once was
squats inside the black cracks:

> [dank dirt floor / lash-shattered / weary-trussed /
> whip-blistered men / sore-bound women / bawling
> babes / moldering grub / festering sleep / dead-
> yoked / dusk toil/ dawn hustle / asking price +
> sugar cane + selling price +orange groves]

I almost miss the historic plaque:
Last Slave Cabin of Buena Esperanza, the Good Hope Plantation.

THE UNITED DAUGHTERS
OF THE CONFEDERACY FLOAT
St. Patrick's Day Parade, Tampa, 2012

*Remember: It is your duty to see that the true history of the South is
presented to future generations.*
Stephen D. Lee, Sons of Confederate Veterans, 1906

I stared from the corner of 7th Avenue and *Avenida de Cuba*
down the block to where the middle-aged belles with faux hoop skirts
and *wish-I-was-in-Dixie* bouffants swayed on a lady-cake float.
Those daughters of the Old South whipped the crowd
into a frenzy for their plastic pearls, flung as the float
hauled itself towards us, beribboned and bedecked
with red-white-and-blue bunting and a backdrop festooned
with the battle flag their kin had vowed never to surrender.

Crammed in with the throng of parade-goers I thought
I saw the 13 stars on the banner of the Lost Cause burst, each
with a lily-white vision to remind me where I came from.
Then as the plantation-on-wheels bore down upon us, listing
beneath the strains of *Way down upon the Suwanee*
and the crowd screamed bloody murder for beads, there issued
a *Boooo!* from out of nowhere that made heads turn for half a second
     Booooo! To the ladies with their ever-pure smiles
        Booo! To heritage and preserving the past
           a *Booo!* that somehow discharged from my mouth
so that the mob stepped back, gave me wide berth as they
reached for the fake treasure
that showered the crowd like grapeshot. I *Booed!*
to beat the band, then glared down to the next block where
another float shifted between the sidewalks in perfect irony.

For there they were
in their dignified blues, the Buffalo Soldiers,
dark as café solo and grinning with their own history,
there they were on their freedom float,
laughing at how sometimes the universe lines things up perfect.
They tossed bushels and bushels of sun-yellow beads
to the mob on the streets that screamed as loud as they'd screamed all night.
And I shut my mouth and I reached.

So Many Hitchhikers on this Street

Nebraska Avenue, Tampa

Just about here everything runs out,
but the women saunter, in the pre-dawn mornings when my kids and I
drive to school, the women out like haunts, until there's straight up sunshine.
Restless, roaming, pacing the broken sidewalks of Nebraska Avenue,
unglamorous, with faces like old mush, mealy-skinned,
bodies bloated, bruised, teeth gone or gray, eyes too bright.
You might think they'd doll up,
but they don't need nothin' fancy to crawl
into some truck that takes the corner quick
 and throws open a door with a rolling stop.
This landmark street, now gutter-dirty,
is a black zipper rusting up the back of our city.
          It was freezing when I glanced into the murkiness
as we drove under the overpass. There stood
a diva from a hip-hop fantasy—glitter-black afro,
thigh-high boots, black lace bustier, and nothing else,
not a thread on between her knees and her waist.
My sons were curled in sleepiness
as we drove on by.
          Once I recognized a hooker I knew.
I saw her across the checkout lanes
in the store where I buy my bread and butter.
I'd seen her trickin', but in the clean light of Publix
I saw her for who she was:
the baby sister of an old, good friend.
Standing in line, she looked like someone
had used her to stub something out.
I remember as a kid she was sweet as white corn and once
after a late football game, as we all rode home at curfew hour,
she put her head on her sister's shoulder and her sister
drew her close and stroked her hair.

NICE 'N' EASY

I think I'm on the road to romance.
With Joe. He's the one that brought the four guys.
Now we're just coasting.
He's the one who saw me in the bathtub.
The other four just swarmed over my old self,
they all just stared at my ratty bra, my big underwear.
Joe was the one who said *Ma'am*, as in
Ma'am, why are you in the bathtub?
And now Joe is saying *breathe, just breathe.*
He's holding my arm and tapping my wrist
and sticking the needle.

Seminole Heights is unraveling under us.
Hillsborough Avenue is just crawling.
Joe's the one that said *yeah*
when the driver said *nice 'n' easy.*
The stretcher slid right on in.
The siren's off. My breathing is rolling
cause I'm one tough broad.
Here I am with Joe,
his little croon over the needle.
Sinatra of the EMT.
Nice 'n' easy does it.
The drip into my veins serenading me.

"ANYTHING HELPS, GOD BLESS"

intersection of Nebraska and Hillsborough Avenues, Tampa

Next time, we'll notice
their Sunday clothes, the orange-yellow vests
that once a week declare to church-goers waiting
at the red light they are keyless. Next to them,
the bundled newspapers like mildewed sheets
in the sun. In rain they are old loaves, piles of fish.
Just once a week, the chairless are allowed
to pack sidewalks and street corners for 12 hours
of unrebuked daylight. Unmolested by bureaucrats,
they swarm through traffic, their vests flapping.
Sometimes a family hawks water
bottles, Dad standing in the gutter holding
a pure spring in each hand, Mom sitting near the cooler,
fanning worry with the lid of a cardboard gift box.
On the bus bench, the kids bend their heads over
math books. Sometimes men with arms like tree
bark and wind-whipped eyes, shuffle up to our
cars, just stand there while our idling motors hum
a weekend song, the cool car air spilling silky and fine.
Mirrorless, maybe they are seers,
holding their scrawled signs, their brains full of
maybe, bellies full of headlines, their vests
like lanterns as they count their days in footsteps,
while we wait for the light at the corner and don't
meet their eyes, right here in the Sunshine State.

WALKING HOME ON HANNA AVENUE, JULY 4TH

He's as wrong as the street's a-shimmer.
Lurching towards heat stroke,
you taste whitening sky,
remember stone roads in Europe
that crowded around you like a pizza oven.
I'm done!
Now here you are walking
through a record noon, stupid in the sun.
Scientific as a heart attack, you think.
You pull the straw hat low,
peer through the weave
like staring through a fence at cool clover.
Something in this heat cooks up a vertigo,
each step taking you one rung up
on the stubborn footstool of everything
dumb you've ever done:
chasing the car as it slid driverless down the hill,
checking the lit gas grill.
Your mamma taught you how to win a fight.
Your eyelashes lit up like sparklers,
eyebrows like scorch marks over your brain.

THE NEXT DOOR NEIGHBOR

2 a.m. work nights, they would slam down aces,
he and the other stringers playing poker at his rusted picnic table,
just beyond our bedroom window.
His black glasses crooked, he'd knock back rye whiskey,
smoke his stupid cigars.
We'd stumble over, sleep-rumpled, plead early alarms.
He never said a word, let the other men mutter or chuckle.
Once, one of them shouted, *Sword Man!*
bent deep into his car trunk until we sidled home.
Other nights he was in his shop, blasting R.E.M at 3:30.
We'd turn our bedroom blinds to slits,
glare towards the hammering light and thrashing yard.
Christmas, he tried hanging lights.
Before we stopped saying hello, we would have helped,
but when we called up the ladder just the back of his head was his reply.

When he first moved in, he'd had a lover.
She refinished the doors, painted murals on the walls.
She laid a dead osprey in the driveway, photographed for art.
Then he sold her things while she visited her mother.
They argued so bad he kicked in glass on his own front door.
All December the panes gaped, blank as a new notebook.
        Even the postman asked me about it:
                Clothes strewn in the ditch. Shadows on his porch.

She took one dog and left.
The other he let howl so long, the chain-link fence shuddered.
He still owns the house, but he's mostly gone.
The house molders.
We saw her at the art show.
Her photos stared when she sidled up, asking, *How is that bad neighbor?*

Four Houses Lost and Returned

[3210] Returned
The oldest house. Black & whites of great grands on the porch, before the war.
He owned a feed store. Eggs, grain, hay.
The little disappeared town of Gary
with a brick schoolhouse folded onto itself.
Train tracks tacking the edge of yard.
Afterwards: the kicked-in door, homeless silhouettes slumped inside.
Yellow clapboard, linen wall cloth, wooden stairs leading up, up, up.
Now a couple's bought it and shored it up.

{3510} Returned
The stuccoed walls. Home movies of uncles on the front steps, home on leave.
Granddaddy's office, his law books stacked up.
The little disappeared town of Gary
where the vegetable man yelled prices from his truck.
Her guava bush and mulberry tree.
In the wall was a loaded gun and a Bible as big as my palm.
Good silver, the chiming clock, wood toys in the closet below the stairs.
Now somebody new will play the baby grand.

<1710> Lost
The first air-conditioner. Polaroids of us on the porch on Halloween.
Distressed wood bookcase in the Florida room.
My parent's closet: his wingtips, her mink.
The postwar neighborhood of Wellswood
where everybody walked to school.
How we'd refill the backyard pool, crank and crank the jalousies.
Kitchen counter, long blue couch, bourbon bottles under the sink.
The terrazzo floors waiting, bare, bare, bare.

(1410) Mine
The big attic. Wedding night video of us on the porch.
Bedroom with French doors undone by the moon.
Plastered-over doorways, the tiny cupboard.
Old-timey neighborhood of Seminole Heights,
where hipsters and hookers shop the same store.
A good ghost creaking the tilting floors, the 1928 bathroom tile.
Beauty bush, laurel oak, old garage giving in to the hum.
My loves smiling back from every frame.

Sanwa International Grocery

i.

Praise to the cart boys, how they corral the runaways
    drifting towards four lanes of traffic on Hillsborough Avenue.
Praise how they trudge to the back lot
    for the once-overloaded, now-abandoned.
Praise how deftly they que them up, tucking each
    into the next like balls into joints.
Praise how they push the heavy line up the incline towards the loading dock,
    how they maneuver the hairpin turn.
        I want to say something magnificent
    about their green T-shirts emblazoned with the orange name.
Praise how they heave and push towards the plastic flaps covering the doors,
    how they clap together their black work gloves as if calling forth
    the magic of dragonfruit, celery root, tomatoes on the vine.

ii

I see a woman in African dress examining prickly pears.
Her breasts are bound tight with a sash.

A man in a green kilt rubs chalk from the winter melons.
Women in turquoise saris peruse the silken tofu.
A Vietnamese family inspects dried lily, lotus root.
Cubans crowd the yucca.
A Chinese gent grabs okra long as a bat.
A lady in hajib wafts around the lentils.

The sugar canes lean together in their bin, deciphering all the languages.
What is carnival cauliflower? How do you cook banana blossom?
I am searching for farro and eggplant.
Take me, says the cactus paddle.
Take me, says the stinky durian.
No us, say stars of rambutan.

When the African woman bends to the fruit, I see her back—
her baby asleep in the binding cloth.

Somewhere Jazz
Paris Street, Tampa

   Trumpet, trumpet flower, and the before
—my body old already, but sparking.
   This was decades before the songs I thought
sang Shadow Garden, the termites, the sirens.
   I wanted this to be about the house,
the ghost that moved the mirror,
the car-in-the-driveway arguments,
late nights waiting up,
slammed & broken glass,
heartbroke pillows.
   But also the oranges before greening,
Spanish moss, old hopes,
money, money and money.
   Our first cat was a tortoise shell
and the bug man said,
She shore is ugly.
   The house where you called down all your ancestors.
   Much before the house I thought was me was thrumming—
pure inside with jazz.

A Note of Thanks

Writing and living poetry is a calling that takes place mostly in the mind, with a bit of spirit and heart thrown in for good measure. Some say it's a lonely calling. But I've not found it so. I've been fortunate to have many supporters and friends to fill my poetry world. First, heartfelt thanks goes to Kimberly Davis for her unwavering enthusiasm for this work and her limitless patience. My sincere gratitude goes to my graduate school and "school of hard knocks" mentors: Stephen Haven, Sandra Beasley, the indefatigable Erica Dawson, whose expert eye and discernment were essential in helping me shape this manuscript, and Peter Meinke, longtime friend who has taught me by example how to live a poet's life with grace. Sincere appreciation goes to my writing colleagues at Saint Leo University, whose ongoing support I treasure: Patrick Crerand, Steven Kistulentz, Anne Barngrover, Brooke King, Carol Ann Moon, Amanda Forrester, Dr. Mary Spoto and, in memoriam, our dear friend and fellow poet Kurt Wilt. To the near-lifetime citizens of my poetry village and everyone in the YellowJacket Press community, especially Susan Lilley, Phyllis McEwen, Silvia Curbelo, Rhonda J. Nelson, Pamela Hill Epps, Mary Jane Ryals, Michael Trammell, Katie Riegel, Gregory Byrd, and my friend and supporter Jenny Carey, cheers and a toast to your steadfastness. Hugs and kisses to my sisters Tina and Felicia Russo, their husbands David Salvador and Kent Foss, and my sons and daughters-in-law, Anthony, Diana, Frank and Jennifer Scaglione for their unwavering encouragement. Finally, to Jeff, my most devoted advocate, most trusted editor, and most beloved, an eternal *yes* to everything. I remain *yours in poetry*.

Notes on the Poems

"American Pantoum": This poem is comprised of lines or parts of lines from newspaper articles about mass shootings that took place in California, Florida and Texas. The poem is dedicated to all American victims of gun violence.

"Did You Find Everything You Need?": On March 22, 2016, "20 people died at the Maelbeek metro station and 130 were wounded, plus 10 more were killed and 100 wounded at Brussels' international airport. The 'working assumption' is that the attackers came from the network behind November's massacres in Paris, which left 130 dead, Belgian security sources said." CNN. Tuesday, March 22, 2016.

"Examining the Cannon" is based on the photograph of GW Bean, PH Cason and Ruoy Cason in 1905 at the Tampa Bay Hotel (now The University of Tampa). Credit: Henry B. Plant Museum Archives.

"Flood Subject": A poet's flood subject is the one to which the poet returns again and again in her work.

"Four Houses Lost and Returned": The first house mentioned in the poem was the home of my maternal great-grandparents and is allegedly the oldest house in Hillsborough County. It was located at 3210 Eighth Avenue until 2017, when it was moved to the Hyde Park neighborhood of Tampa.

"From Sea to Shining": The poem uses nouns, verbs and adjectives from "America the Beautiful" in the same order in which they appear in the song.

"I Have Monkeys": This poem takes poetic license with my maternal grandfather's possible involvement with the Ku Klux Klan who were active and somewhat prominent in Tampa in the early 20th century. While there is no proof that my grandfather was a member, there is proof that when he ran for office on the city commission, he claimed their endorsement. The italicized line near the end of the poem is a quote attributed to John Scopes. When he was asked if he would stand a test case in court on the teaching of evolution 'He later explained his decision: "the best time to scotch the snake is when it starts to wiggle."'http://law2.umkc.edu/faculty/projects/ftrials/scopes/evolut.htm. 4 August 2015.

"Nebraska Avenue Torch Song": The white plaster cat still clings to the roof of Adams and Jennings Funeral Home on the corner of Nebraska and Sligh Avenues, Tampa.

"Old Orange Avenue": Old Orange Avenue is a stand-in for Tampa's storied Central Avenue, often called the Harlem of the South for hosting the top black entertainers in the nation.

"Old Orange Avenue" and "Old South Carriage Tours" part iii: Information about the riots in Tampa can be found in the article "Racism in Tampa boiled over 50 years ago into Central Avenue riots," published in the *Tampa Bay Times*, June 7, 2017. http://www.tampabay.com/news/humaninterest/racism-in-tampa-boiled-over-50-years-ago-into-central-avenue-riots/2326360

"Pecha Kucha for Big Guava": Burgert Brothers prints Courtesy, Tampa-Hillsborough County Public Library System. http://digitalcollections.hcplc.org/cdm/landingpage/collection/p15391coll1 According to *Lynching and Establishment Violence in Tampa, 1858-1935* by Robert P. Ingalls there were at least seven lynchings that took place in Tampa at the turn of the 20th century.

"Please Help This Vet": On April 30, 1975. Saigon fell to the forces of North Vietnam and thousands of "at risk" Vietnamese joined Americans still left in Vietnam to be evacuated by the largest helicopter evacuation in history (Operation Frequent Wind). Wikipedia.

"Sanwa International Grocery" section i is loosely inspired by "For the Sleepwalkers" by Edward Hirsch.

About the Author

Gianna Russo is a Tampa native and third generation Floridian. She is the author of *Moonflower*, winner of the Florida Book Award Bronze and Florida Publishers Association Silver awards. A Pushcart Prize nominee, she has had publications in *Green Mountains Review*, *The Sun*, *Poet Lore*, *The MacGuffin*, *Tampa Review*, *Valparaiso*, *Ekphrasis*, *Crab Orchard Review*, *Florida Review*, *Florida Humanities Council Forum*, *Water Stone*, *Karamu*, *The Bloomsbury Review*, and *Calyx*, among others. She is founding editor of the Florida poetry chapbook publisher YellowJacket Press. She holds an MFA in Poetry from The University of Tampa. She is Assistant Professor of English and Creative Writing at Saint Leo University where she directs the Sandhill Writers Retreat.

. . . continued from page ii.

Gianna Russo creates a feast for the senses in her gorgeously rich collection, *One House Down.* The book begins with a neighborhood's midnight peace shattered by a lovers' quarrel, then careens thrillingly though the jasmine and magnolia-scented streets of Tampa, Florida with dissonant echoes of cigar rollers and Jim Crow, Gasparilla queens and school shooter training. It's all here: the cool terrazzo floors and cherry martinis alongside okra and banana blossom, motel roach powder, and cops folding women like burritos into their squad cars. Russo lures us into a world both lush and concrete, her truths as insistent as the thudding bass in a passing car.

—Susan Lilley, First Poet Laureate of Orlando, Florida
and author of *Venus in Retrograde.*

Waltzing alone on one page, doing the cha-cha with a partner on another, Gianna Russo tangoes from corner to corner, crossing the unreachable-reach, a darkened ballroom. Twisting and turning, this poet's words turn the lightson, casting honest daylight upon the nightmares of our times. *One House Down* tells a her-story in compelling rhythms, dramatic compression, but also accommodates the necessary distillation, jazz.

—Earl Sherman Braggs, author of *Negro Side of the Moon*

Gianna Russo's poems in *One House Down* remind me of searchlights casting about the sordid and beautiful in equal measure. With a keen eye and clear narrative, the voice behind these poems hangs tight to everyday experience, the shadowy spaces reminding us we're always at ". . . the intersection of heartbreak and wanting more." There are "hipsters and hookers" in these pages, "grace notes of cicadas" and sudden violence—everywhere the nuance of a question: "What does it take to do good in this world?" These poems are too honest to try to answer this question for us. Instead, looking straight at our human flaws, with warmth and generosity Gianna challenges us to "wake and drive our lives into the answer," and I'm guessing with all our windows down.

—Helen Wallace, Poet Laureate of Saint Petersburg, Florida
and author of *Shimming the Glass House*

CPSIA information can be obtained
at www.ICGtesting.com
Printed in the USA
FFHW021938111019
55483837-61306FF